Healing Haikus

A Poetic Prescription for Surviving Cancer

D1414073

Marjorie Miles, DCH, MFT

Foreword by Sharon Bray, Ed.D.

"This material is intended to provide general
information to you. Consult your health
care professional with any questions relating
to a medical problem or condition."

This book is not intended as a substitute for the medical
advice of physicians. The reader should regularly consult a
physician in matters relating to his/her health and
particularly with respect to any symptoms that may require
diagnosis or medical attention.

Printed in the United States of America

First Printing, 2013

ISBN-13: 978-1493512065

ISBN-10: 1493512064

Library of Congress Control Number: 2013921241
CreateSpace Independent Publishing PlatformNorth
Charleston, South Carolina

Table of Contents

This Book is Dedicated To

My mother and father who gave me life
My husband, Ben, who helped save it
And my family and friends who enrich it

And

Anyone Who Has Been Touched by Cancer

Foreword

A cancer diagnosis, as Marjorie Miles shows us in *Healing Haikus*, often precipitates a kind of identity crisis. Not only does it seem as if your body has betrayed you, but you're confronted with a multitude of powerful, sometimes conflicting, emotions. Your life is turned upside down, inside out, and the self you took for granted is nowhere to be found. "Why me?" You might ask. "Why me?"

When you become a cancer patient, you cling to every ray of hope that you will be cured. You fight against the fears that threaten to overtake you in the dark hours of night. You willingly accept any reassurance your doctors can offer; you seek alternate opinions, looking for the best possible outcome. As you struggle to stay steady in the maelstrom of diagnoses, surgeries, chemotherapies, and radiation treatments, you invest your doctors and their medicines with magical powers. Yet even if you are "cured" of cancer, does it make you whole again? As Arthur Frank reminds us in his memoir, *At the Will of the Body,* "When the body breaks down, so does life. Medicine may fix the body, but it doesn't put one's life back together."

What helps you heal once the crisis has passed? How do you pick up the pieces of your shattered self and make yourself whole again?

When life hurts, the research shows, writing can help. Marjorie Miles' book provides testimony to the healing power of writing, discovered as she sat in her physician's office and was compelled to transform her experience into a poetic form, haiku.

Why haiku? Even to the most timid of writers, it is a form that is easily accessible. Simple in form and structure, it gets to the essence of a moment and results in surprising insights about what we observe, whether in nature or ourselves. "Every haiku," Joel Weishaus writes in *The Healing Spirit of Haiku,* "is a prescription for a larger life." Haiku offers the writer a shorthand way of capturing a moment, an emotion *and* making sense of it—all in three short lines, as Marjorie Miles shows us.

Haikus hold feelings
Beyond our word descriptions
Divine containers

The essence of haiku lies in its visual intensity. It paints a picture in the readers' mind, calling attention to an observation *and* a story hinted at behind the image. Imagery, in any kind of expressive writing, is closely intertwined with emotions. Imagery weaves together the body, mind and spirit. For example, consider this haiku written by Richard Moss, MD:

The bird's darting flight
Insects caught for hungry mouths
Death renewing life

But a poem like haiku does even more for us. As Jane Hirshfield, Chancellor of the American Academy of Poets, recently stated, "any creative expression draws from the world and leads outward, back into the world...And so, it's no surprise that the Japanese haiku poet Basho, even during his

final illness in 1694, might wonder about his neighbor's fate"
(www.poets.org, September 2013):

deep autumn--
my neighbor,
how is he doing?

Writing, whether prose or poetry, is a vessel for creative self-expression, but in sharing our poems and stories with one another, others may be inspired to find their voices and share their own stories of illness and healing. Haiku offers a deceptively powerful way to communicate our experiences—and to help us heal.

A haiku poem is simple and straightforward in form--three lines, the first containing five syllables, the second, seven, and the third, five, for a total of seventeen syllables—but there is nothing simple in its power to capture the heart of our experiences with life. Haiku conveys images *and* a theme that unites them. It teaches us the power of observation *and* meaning-making. It invites us to do more than simply observe; writing a haiku takes us inside ourselves, helps us become aware of the feelings evoked by what we see and experience. Writing a haiku is truly a meditation, a container for quiet, calm and focus, something Marjorie Miles explains in her introduction:

I was building an interior
place within myself where
I could rest, find comfort,
hear my intuitive voice...
Through these simple
three line poems, I
...discovered a sacred
place for reflecting and

processing the fast-paced
proliferation of events ...
set in motion by my
cancer diagnosis.

Writing haiku gives you a simple, yet beautiful way to express your journey through cancer and into healing. In *Healing Haikus*, Marjorie Miles offers us an intimate glimpse into her cancer journey, and in doing so, invites the reader to travel along, from diagnosis, surgery, treatments, and into the re-discovery of joy and wholeness. Travel along with her, reader, and discover the healing power of haiku.

Sharon Bray, Ed.D.
Author of *When Words Heal, Writing Through Cancer* (2007) and
A Healing Journey, Writing Together Through Breast Cancer (2004)
www.writingthroughcancer.com

My muse was silenced

Neglect had stifled her voice

But cancer heard her

Introduction

"It's cancer." Those two words change your life forever.

You begin a trek into uncharted territory filled with boulders of fear, waves of uncertainty, and mountains of overwhelm. While attempting to find footing in the swiftly moving river of information, you are urged to make important treatment decisions.

I know...because I have made the journey from diagnosis, surgery, chemotherapy, and radiation to recuperation and healing.

I am a cancer survivor.

On that road from illness to recovery, the last thing I expected to encounter was a *Poetry Muse*—an inspirational traveling companion—carrying a suitcase filled with healing words and a prescription for recovering Self expression.

In classical Greek mythology there was not only one muse, but nine. They are the daughters of Zeus and Mnemosyne who preside over and inspire each of several branches of literature, art, history and science—three of the Muses are specifically dedicated to poetry—epic, love and sacred poetry. Other definitions of a muse include a guiding spirit, a source of an artist's inspiration and a poet.

My Poetry Muse arrived as a guiding spirit who led me to an ancient form of Japanese poetry called haiku. Through poem-making, I discovered the ultimate call of the muses. It is to live your life creatively and authentically.

As a trained counselor and clinical hypnotherapist, I learned about the power of words to create positive feelings, change behavior and promote healing. While recovering from cancer, I discovered that poetry's similar hypnotic language could accomplish those results...and more.

Haikus—short 3-line poems consisting of 17 syllables—became sacred containers for the spectrum of my feelings ranging from sadness, anxiety and anger to gratitude, humor and hope. Even my darkest feelings about loss, mortality, and the specter of death found a place here for their voices to be heard.

Haikus hold feelings

Beyond our word descriptions

Divine containers

Writing haiku poetry offered me a safe haven where I could rest, recuperate and reflect. Prior to my becoming ill, the expressive parts of me had become lost under the demands of everyday living. As a young girl, I had exhibited a talent for drawing—but this gift disappeared when I grew older. I had acted in Community Theater when I was in my 30's, but after a few years I stopped, because it was too time-consuming.

When I began writing this book, a submerged memory surfaced. I recalled another creative time in my life. Before transitioning from a psychotherapist to college professor, I had worked as a writer for a company called Soaps by Phone! I had been hired to write a synopsis for each of the five ABC television soap operas that were airing daily. My summary scripts were recorded by a professional radio announcer, and accessed through an 800 Telephone Number by subscribers who had missed the current day's episode.

I had *completely forgotten* my experience as a writer ...until cancer called it back.

While waiting in my doctor's office, I heard an inner voice instructing me to write a haiku. *What could possibly be poetic about cancer?* Despite my skepticism, I began writing. Within moments, the words tumbled from my pen, and my first healing haiku appeared on the page. The poem was about radiation treatment, and I read it aloud. Each of the 17 syllables reverberated within me and found a subterranean place of remembrance. These 3 lines unearthed my buried creative expression and sparked a journey back to wholeness. That night I purchased a journal, and the next day I began a morning ritual of writing *daily h*aikus. At first, these poems voiced only my experience with cancer, but later they revealed a much larger story.

My deepest wish for you, dear reader, is that by sharing my story and haiku poetry, *you* will discover a deeper meaning in the cancer experience, strengthen the healing process, and set free your own creative voice.

Let's begin...but before you turn the page, take a moment to imagine that we are holding each other's hands...as we leave the familiar and travel the terrain called cancer.

Chapter 1

Listening to My Inner Voice
You Talking to Me?

In June 2010, I was diagnosed with lung cancer. I had surgery to remove the lower portion of my left lung, followed by chemotherapy. It was during the final phase of my treatment—radiation—when something unexpected happened.

While waiting in my radiologist's office, I began daydreaming. In that gauzy, gossamer state of consciousness between waking and sleeping, I heard the Voice.

Simply and clearly, it said: "You need to write a poem."

"You've got to be kidding. *This* doesn't feel very poetic!" I snapped back.

Ignoring me, the Voice continued, "And the poem should be a *haiku!*"

"A *what*?"

"I am *not* a poet," I grumbled.

Yet, I began writing...and the haiku formula—five syllables in the first line, seven syllables in the second line, and five syllables in the last line—found its way to the scrap of paper I had been holding.

Something powerful, mysterious and incomprehensible had just occurred.

When my oncology radiologist opened the door and entered the room, he startled me back to full consciousness. He had been detained at a meeting and apologized for arriving late to our appointment. Although I knew he was pressed for time, I felt compelled to tell him, "I just wrote a poem...about radiation... and I would love to read it to you."

Imagine how thrilled he was to hear this news. After furtively glancing at his watch, he submitted to my request and patiently listened to me read the haiku aloud for the first time.

Radiation...Zap!
Search and find the mutant cells
Glowing...going...GONE

Inexplicably, I found myself performing the haiku with hand gestures—including a loud clap on the last syllable and the last word, GONE!

For what seemed like a long time, we just stared at one another. Finally, the doctor broke the silence. With a voice filled with emotion, he said, "May I have a copy? I want to share this with my other patients."

It was during that exchange between my doctor and me that I realized the healing power of poetry. Writing poetry, I concluded, was more than scribbling words on a blank page. A haiku could transform itself into a container for the essence of the human spirit—despite the body's vulnerability—and communicate that core to another human being.

Later that day, I read my poem (hand gestures and all) to my husband, Ben. The words touched him, too.

"I have an idea," Ben said. "Challenge yourself to write three of these haiku daily."

"Okay," I agreed, completely unaware that Ben's suggestion would prove life-altering

Could writing haiku help me make some sense out of this cancer experience? Would this help me discover more about the Voice and why it chose to speak to me at this time?

After I began my haiku writing practice, I learned that I wasn't just using words to create a poem. I was building an interior place within myself where I could rest, find comfort, hear my intuitive voice—and eventually recover my creative expression. Through these simple three line poems, I also discovered a sacred place for reflecting and processing the fast-paced proliferation of events that had been set in motion by my cancer diagnosis.

Recovering my own artistic voice—and helping others to find theirs through expressive writing—has been transformative and is the guiding force for writing this book.

Chapter 2

The Accident...And the Discovery
Where's My Stunt Double?

It all began as a minor distraction.

As I was walking down the staircase at home, I attempted to read some mail I was holding in my hand. I missed a step and fought to remain upright. My feet frantically searched for something solid, but touched only empty space. When I landed, the left side of my body collided with the corner of a wooden chair at the bottom of the stairs. Then I fell backwards onto the hard, cold tile entrance way. Sprawled on my back, I decided not to move until I could access my condition. However, an incoming phone call began screaming for my attention. I rolled over slowly until I was on my knees and, like an old woman plagued with arthritis, I rose to my feet. Taking small baby steps, I walked towards the insistent r-r-r-r—ing...r-r-r-r—ing...r-r-r—ing emanating from across the room.

When I finally reached the telephone, I spoke haltingly and breathlessly into the receiver, "H-h-hello?"

My husband, Ben, had meant to call a friend, but he misdialed and reached our home telephone number instead. He was surprised to hear *my* voice answer his call.

Angels push...I fall

Bottom of stairs...rib seems hurt

Phone rings...a *mistake?*

"What's wrong?" he said.

"I slipped and fell down the stairs." Attempting to downplay the situation, I continued, "But it was only a few steps."

Talking into the phone's mouthpiece and still moving slowly, I headed for the refrigerator. "I think I'll put just a bag of frozen peas on it."

"I think you should go to the chiropractor," Ben countered.

"It's late. The traffic is going to be a mess. I'll be fine," I argued.

"I'm coming home, Ben insisted. "I'll be there in a few minutes to take you there myself."

The finality of my husband's declaration ended the discussion, and (what I now refer to as my *Angel Push)* had also started us on the journey to my cancer diagnosis.

Ben maneuvered our car through the thickening rush hour traffic, and we finally arrived at my chiropractor's office. A few minutes later, I was lying on an exam table reciting the details of my fall and describing the soreness I was still feeling around my left side.

Tenderly, the doctor touched the area where I felt bruised. I was starting to feel a little better, when he registered concern about working on me any further.

"You might have a broken a rib," he said. "I'd like you to get an X-ray before I do anything else."

Oh crap! I thought. *Everyone is making a big deal out of this. I'm tired and hungry, and I just want to go home. Now we need to drive somewhere else?*

Hoping for a reprieve, I reminded my chiropractor that it was nearly 5 o'clock.

Unwavering, he called ahead and got assurances that everyone at the imaging facility would remain there until 6 o'clock.

They were expecting me.

Ben and I arrived at our destination just as one of the staff members was about to close the office door. I filled out some forms and was ushered into another room. The X-rays were taken, and I was told that the radiologist would fax my results that night to my chiropractor.

So Ben and I returned to the chiropractor's office and waited for the radiology report. An hour and half later, we were told the news I had expected: No broken rib.

Terrific! Now we can go home and eat. I'm starving...

We scheduled a routine follow-up appointment with my chiropractor for the next day. Even though I was feeling much better in the morning, Ben insisted I keep the appointment and volunteered to drive me, again.

My chiropractor's eyes were downcast when he greeted us. Gripping the manila folder he held in his hand, he suggested that both Ben and I join him in his private office.

He explained that the radiologist had called him back because the X-ray had revealed something on my left lung. I remember hearing the words "found a mass" and seeing the doctor's lips moving soundlessly afterwards. His remaining words were obliterated by thoughts in my head.

Shocking news—a mass!

A large one hidden from view

What should I do now?

Immediately, Ben and I made an appointment with my primary care physician. Several hours later, we left her office with a referral to a different doctor.

This was all happening too fast! One appointment was blurring into another.

The following day, Ben and I were seated in a small stuffy office across the desk from a pulmonary specialist. After examining me and reviewing my X-rays, he announced the necessity for yet another appointment.

This one was for a biopsy.

Chapter 3

Lions and Tigers and Biopsies, Oh My!
The Land Beyond X-rays

For some life-changing events, you get an early warning. Weather reports caution about storm fronts heading your way, or you receive a notification that your company will be "down-sizing" in a month.

Then there are those times when a seismic experience rocks your inner Richter scale. A biopsy is one of those incidents where you find yourself completely unprepared, and your very foundation is shaken.

A health-conscious vegetarian for decades, I exercised daily and considered myself in good physical health. It was inconceivable to me that a "mass" could be discovered in my left lung.

I jokingly told friends and family that the so-called "mass" was probably the thumbprint of the technician who took the X-ray, and soon the mistake would be rectified.

Sick was not a word that I could even entertain.

Having a biopsy would clear this all up. *Yes, it certainly would.*

Biopsy and scans

Needles and pictures will tell

More of *real* story

The actual biopsy was a blur. Although my recollection of this outpatient procedure is vague, I do remember the small room in which several medical personnel and I were gathered. Their instructions and demeanor were precise and professional, and their collective, clinical movements seemed

34

as if they had been choreographed. Swiftly and expertly, I was hooked up to an I.V. Next I was instructed to lie down with my left side up. A soft spoken technician said, "We are going to give you a local anthestetic, so you will not feel any pain. There will be a loud clicking sound—similar to that made by a stapler—but you will only feel a sense of pressure, no pain, when the needle is inserted."

I averted my eyes from the large hypodermic I had spotted with my peripheral vision. Instead, I fixed my gaze on my hand which was holding a smiling photograph of Ben. During the process, I gripped his picture tightly and stared into Ben's big, comforting and loving blue eyes—blocking out everything else around me.

I had read somewhere that if you looked into a loved one's face during a potentially painful treatment or intervention, the discomfort would be minimized. It worked so well that I have few additional memories about the actual procedure.

Waiting for the biopsy report was both a tortuous event and a blessed reprieve.

After all no news is good news. Right?

I continued to comfort myself by thinking: *I have no symptoms—a barely noticeable, occasional cough (probably dust allergies or pollen) and some fatigue (most likely from everyday stress).*

Those and other thoughts racing through my mind became both a silent chant and fervent prayer. *"I am fine...I am fine..I am fine"*.

This is some kind of macabre mistake.

The *Unthinkable*

Push those thoughts out of my mind

Wait for test results

Chapter 4

The Diagnosis
I Did Not Audition for This Role

My dear friend, Teena, volunteered to go with Ben and me to the next appointment with the pulmonologist. Not only was she there for moral support, but she offered "another set of ears" to hear about the findings of the biopsy. If the news was good, we could collectively exhale and celebrate my good fortune with one another. If the news was bad, we could find solace with one another and piece together the bits of information we were each able to grasp about the diagnosis, and possible treatment.

I recommend bringing another person—a spouse, partner, family member, or friend—to all your doctors' appointments. Think of this person as your medical liaison. Select someone who can listen well, take notes, and ask appropriate questions. In other words, seek a comforting, competent medical advocate.

Sitting side-by-side in the small, cramped doctor's office, Ben, Teena and I attempted to calm our anxiety and frayed nerves by filling the air with idle chatter. My thoughts kept wandering from our conversation and the feeble smiles we gave to one another—all futile attempts at distraction.

What's taking so long? Isn't the doctor aware of the emotional toll this intermittable waiting is taking?

When the doctor arrived, he was holding an official looking file in his hands. As he unsheathed the document, I thought hopefully, "*...and the Winner is...*"

All hope vanished as he uttered the word, "malignant".

"*Cancer?*" I asked, incredulous.

"Yes, it's cancer," the doctor answered matter-of-factly. His eyes remained on the report. "We spoke about that possiblity".

Hell, no we didn't. I would have remembered. *Wouldn't I?*

That simple, horrifying declaration: **"You have cancer"** continued to reverberate in my head. *What?!* A moment ago, I was healthy Marjorie Miles. Suddenly, all the familiar perceptions surrounding *who I thought I was* immediately vaporized. I was now a **patient.**

Without emotion

Doctor says, "It *is* cancer."

It can't be...NOT me!

Chapter 5

We're Talking Surgery?
I Hate This Dialogue

Disoriented, I felt both my mind and body tighten to absorb the shock. Fear, sadness, anger and a flood of other emotions threatened to push through the walls of my defenses.

Happening too fast!

Feeling so vulnerable

Brace for the unknown...

While I was still attempting to process my diagnosis, more words continued to tumble out of the doctor's mouth.

Oh no! Is he saying something about surgery?

A fierce part of me wanted that unwelcome, cancerous tumor out of me NOW. If I could have reached into my chest and pulled it out with my bare hands in the doctor's office, I would have.

Another part of me (I was beginning to feel a bit like Sybil— the woman who was diagnosed with more than 20 distinct personalities) projected myself into the near future, suffering the pain from incisions, tubes, and suture removal.

Even one wildly irrational part me imagined going to Brazil, changing my identity, and *tricking* the cancer into thinking I was someone else.

Decisions need to be made quickly. I don't think I'm up to this!

I corralled my errant thoughts and extended my hand to accept the list of surgeon referrals the pulmonologist handed

to me.   My movements were similar to a robot, as I put
names of the recommended doctors into my purse.

No time to process

Surgeons to be contacted

Choose who will cut me

Despite my outer composure, I felt as though I had just
heard the tinkling sounds that windows make just before the
earth shifts violently.

As we left the medical building, I looked into the nearly
expressionless faces of Ben and Teena—who were valiantly
hiding their own shock and fear.

Still reeling from the news of my diagnosis, I was definitely not in any condition to begin the task of contacting potential surgeons for an appointment.

Thank heavens for Ben.

Later that day, and for several days after my doctor's appointment, Ben became singularly focused. He sat, tirelessly, hour after hour, hunched at our computer—clicking steadfastly on the keyboard—learning all he could about lung cancer and thoracic surgeons.

Online research is an especially good task for your medical advocate. It keeps them focused on positive, helpful and necessary actions, while giving the "patient" some much needed safe, sacred emotional space.

However, I suggest using the internet, judiciously, because it can prove to be a double-edged sword.

While researching online can be extremely helpful in finding a good surgeon (like it did in my case), I do not recommend spending too much time online reading about the type of cancer you have—especially statistics. _You are NOT a statistic!_ It's very easy to find yourself accidentally meandering through websites and forums where people are discussing the world's worst case scenarios. Not only is this not helpful, but it will raise your fear levels off the charts. Gather just enough information to guide you in effective decision-making.

Determined to find the best surgeon for my diagnosis, Ben continued to disappear for endless stretches of time behind the closed door of our home office. It seemed like every spare moment, he was Googling, clicking, and reading about doctors and procedures.

Eureka!

Ben excitedly told me about a surgeon he had discovered on the internet who was an expert in performing Video-Assisted Thoracic Surgery (VATS). This minimally invasive procedure involved removing the lower left lobe of my lung through several small incisions on my side and under my breast.

Ben searches for hours

Finds specialty-trained doctor

Can take mass from side

After a brief discussion, Ben and I dismissed the list of traditional thoracic surgeons on the referral sheet from the pulmonologist. Instead, we scheduled a consultation appointment with the VATS doctor.

The VATS surgeon's office staff was warm and welcoming. I felt reassured by the doctor's hearty handshake and smiling eyes, as he ushered Ben and me into his office. Although he was dressed casually in typical Southern California garb, there was nothing casual in the way he scrutinized and assessed my CAT scan and X-rays. Afterwards, he patiently explained how I would be a good candidate for the VATS procedure.

I was very impressed with the surgeon's level of expertise, the thoroughness of his answers to our myriad questions and his quick humor. Ben and I felt relieved that we had found a good doctor.

However—before I made a decision about who would perform the operation—I was encouraged to get a second opinion.

The VATS surgeon was amenable.
Good sign, I thought.

My brother, Bill, and I have a close and supportive relationship. Although he lives on the opposite coast from me in North Carolina, we maintain contact through emails, phone calls and Skype. When Bill learned about my cancer diagnosis and the need for surgery, he volunteered to find another referral for me. An Associate Clinical Professor in Psychiatry at Duke University Medical Center, Bill was accustomed to interacting with doctors and medical personnel. After expressing his concerns about my situation to several of his colleagues, Bill received the name of a well-respected thoracic surgeon, affiliated with a famous teaching hospital in Los Angeles.

Although this doctor's office was a 100 mile round trip from our home, Ben and I were committed to the finding the most skilled surgeon and the best possible outcome. So a few days later, we were inching through the crowded California Freeway traffic to yet another appointment.

As soon as I entered the clinic-like setting in the huge teaching hospital where the surgeon was located, I felt more like a number than a person. Emotionally and physically exhausted from all my previous medical appointments, I resented having to fill out an extensive questionnaire requesting all of my medical history, records, and "reason for this visit" AGAIN. Before I was permitted to talk with the surgeon, his physician's assistant screened my paperwork, discussed my diagnosis, and then explained the doctor's surgical protocol.

The physician's assistant told me that I would require two surgeries. The first surgery would entail an incision into the mediastinum to determine if the cancer had spread to the lymph nodes.

After hearing the words "two surgeries", the physician's assistant's dispassionate and lifeless voice sounded like the pesky buzz that an irritating fly makes when it dive-bombs around your ear.

After all, I could only take so much information at a time, and it was all beginning to sound just awful.

The long-awaited surgeon finally arrived. Walking quickly, he breezed confidently into the office. Dressed in a crisp, white lab coat—adorned by a stethoscope at the neckline—he looked like a doctor straight from central casting. A dour, pinched expression fixed on his lips made him appear as though he had just tasted something unpleasant.

I'll bet his Funny Bone was removed in childhood, I thought ruefully.

Quelling my initial critical judgments, I chastised myself: *He's not here to win the "Doctor Congeniality Award." Just stay focused on assessing his knowledge, expertise, and skills.*

But, frankly, when this guy started speaking about the traditional thoracic procedure he wanted to perform and the amount of time for my recovery, he scared me. Speaking like a battlefield general on the eve of a massive attack, this doctor's objectives became quite clear. He would kill every one of those damn cancer cells—regardless of any collateral damage to the rest of me.

He's talking about opening my chest, cracking ribs—maybe even removing one of them. Yikes!!!

Seeking more in depth answers and possible options, I questioned the necessity of two surgeries and the invasiveness of the second. The surgeon responded by impugning the VATS doctor's ability to remove such a large tumor (approximately the size of a fist) from between my immovable ribs—and accusing me of being vain!

I was stunned speechless. The walls seemed to move closer, and I felt claustrophobic in this man's presence. Tears were welling in my eyes, and the top of my head felt hot.

I was extremely grateful when the doctor brought the consultation—and interrogation—to an abrupt close. Feeling more anxious than I had been earlier that day, I ran to the elevator and pressed the Ground Floor button. Once outside, I breathed in deep gulps of fresh air.

Ben and I collectively sighed as soon as we were back in our car...heading home. During the lengthy drive, we began discussing our confusion and concerns with one another.

Is tumor too big?

Do ribs need to be broken?

Can VATS work for me?

Then Ben suggested that I phone the VATS surgeon and make another appointment with him to get clarification and answers to our new questions. I placed the call on my cell phone, and the empathetic VATS doctor offered us his last appointment of the day.

We drove—as fast as Los Angeles traffic nearing rush hour allowed—straight to the physician's office.

Despite my feelings about the other surgeon and the procedures he discussed, I was glad that I sought a second opinion. I now had criteria and more data for asking better questions and for making an informed decision about who would operate on me.

The VATS doctor answered all my questions, making my choice of surgeons easier.

Can squish lung like sponge

Done this with bigger tumors

Just one surgery

Okay...I've made my selection. The envelope, please...ahem...The VATs Doctor!

What a relief.

But not long lasting.

Now that I had selected a surgeon, the operation had become a reality. As a result, I would be assuming more of my unfamiliar and unwanted role—patient.

I scheduled the date for my surgery. As I entered July 28, 2010 on my calendar, my body involuntarily shuddered—as if I were standing under the spray of an icy cold shower.

Chapter 6

Preparing for the "Grand Adventure"
Lights...Camera...Action!

I had been putting off the inevitable. There were certain people with whom I still needed to share the news of my diagnosis and upcoming surgery.

Having already told most of my family about my diagnosis, I decided not to burden my 91 year old mother, who lives in an extended care community, with my situation. I wanted to spare her unnecessary worry; and, truthfully, I felt too emotionally fragile to handle both of our feelings. Selfishly, I needed all my energies focused on what was ahead of me.

I chose selectively to share my health challenges with those friends and colleagues who were healers and/or spiritually-minded, positive thinkers. I avoided telling anyone who might exhibit one of those pitiful, hang-dog faces, regale me with horror stories about all the people they knew who had died of cancer, or advise me about the latest coffee enema treatment.

My friends and family to whom I revealed my diagnosis and upcoming surgery did not disappoint me. They all rallied and offered their invaluable support every step of the journey.

Avoid "gloom and doom"

Only positive people

Family and friends

There was really little time to process what was happening, but I did find several things that provided some solace.

Humor, prayers, and love

A recipe for healing

To chase away fears

To keep my spirits up, I used humor and positive language to describe and reframe my experience. Instead of talking about my upcoming surgery, I spoke about my *Grand Adventure* into new uncharted territory and about how outrageously chic I needed to be outfitted for this trek.

Big Adventure starts...

Don pith helmet and boa

Flask of scotch (I wish)

Shortly after my announcement about how I should dress for my surgery, a precious pink boa arrived in the mail.

A few days later, another caring friend sent me a personally, hand-crafted "pith helmet." Her humorous protective hat was an oversized football helmet—overflowing with glued flowers and feathers—and a drinking straw cleverly attached to hidden cup holders (for an adult beverage).

I also discovered a pink magic wand nestled discretely inside the same package.

Pith Helmet Created by Judy Ranieri

Friends and family continued to surprise me with additional and frequent *care packages* that delighted and comforted me: a gift subscription for Netflix, hand-sewn clothes for recovery comfort, a soft nap blanket and nap socks to keep me warm, get-well wishes, drawings, pins, jewelry and good luck totems.

Day of Surgery

Feels like it will never come

Arrives too quickly

On June 28, 2010 I packed my chosen gear, and Ben and I headed for the hospital.

Since I have always despised those homely, one-size-fits-all hospital gowns, I made sure my pink boa accessory was in my small suitcase.

Additionally, I had packed a powerful, uplifting picture that my artist friend, Debbie Hart, had painted. It depicted me

61

wearing a hospital gown, a pink boa, and a queenly crown. Standing behind a re-envisioned hospital bed, Archangels Michael and Raphael had my back.

"Marjorie with Archangels Michael and Raphael"
Artist Debbie Hart

These touchstones were invaluable to me—especially when I began the dreary Admittance Procedure—and when I woke from surgery.

Fill out reams of forms

Meet people who prepare you

Put on "patient" garb

SURGERY

Without makeup, wearing a one-size-fits-all hospital gown and a shower cap on my head, I was a vision of loveliness for the all medical personnel swarming around me. While intravenous hookups were inserted into my arm, I was completing forms and answering questions. The anesthesiologist stopped by my cubicle and introduced himself. He was followed by my surgeon who joked with me and drew surgical marks my left side.

Moments later, I said my "goodbyes" to Ben and Teena.

It was show time.

Needles pushed in veins

Rolled on gurney through long halls

Lights bright...ceilings white...

While I was being wheeled into the operating room, I vaguely remembered something that my surgeon had told me...*listen for...a gurgling sound...that chest tubes make when they have been inserted...that means that the tumor was operable.*

What is there to say about surgery—except for the best part— you are *unconscious* during the entire procedure.

My left lobe *taken*

Cameras and scalpels pierce...

Hoses and stitches xxxxxxxxxxxx

My chest swathed in bandages and my arm still hooked up to an I.V. line hanging from a pole, I floated back into consciousness. I immediately felt the ache in my left side and heard the sound of someone's voice becoming more audible.

Oh *no! I don't hear any gurgling noises. What happened?*

I groggily opened my eyes and glanced down at my body, and there it was—a chest tube protruding from my side.

Wake up...it's over!

Relief...chest tubes inside...PAIN!

Begin the healing

Was the news good? I thought so.

Surgery went well

Margins around tumor clear

Await more results...

POST SURGERY

My pain was managed and minimized, and everyone who entered my room (and there seemed to be an ongoing parade) introduced themselves and explained what they were going to do.

After an appropriate length of time of just lying around (I think it was several hours after the operation), I was helped to my feet by a nurse and instructed to move.

Up and out of bed

Laps around hospital floor

I.V.'s stroll with me

For the next few days, medical staff, dietary aides, and volunteers made regular appearances. Additionally, a flurry of visitors, phone calls, and flowers arrived.

I felt surrounded by love and caring attention. Rest, though, was nearly impossible.

People in and out

Modesty not welcome here

Male nurse gives me bath

Amazingly, four days after undergoing my operation, I was being prepared to go home. It was a welcome thought— mixed with feelings of trepidation.

My VATS surgeon arrived for a final hospital visit. After examining his expert handiwork, he pulled out the protruding chest tube and stitched up the small gap left in its place—all with one hand!

Pull out all the tubes

"Take a deep breath and let go"

More stitches put in

During my hospital stay my sister-in-law, Jackie, sent me a beautiful edible bouquet of mouth-watering fresh fruits, accompanied by a soft, huggable teddy bear. It was a most generous and loving gift.

So, it was completely unexpected when she phoned and also *volunteered* to travel to Southern California to stay with Ben and me during the several anxiety-ridden days that would accompany my return home. Relieved that someone would be home with me when Ben returned to work the following day, I felt even more secure in the knowledge that Jackie was a trained medical professional.

Jackie flies down here

Reassuring...she's a nurse

Help for me at home

I still find it difficult to express my gratitude for her selfless act and gracious support.

If possible, I recommend arranging for additional help from a relative, friend, or neighbor to assist you and your caregiver (if you are fortunate to be living with one) during the first couple of days of this physically and emotionally demanding time period.

Although I was happy to be home again, I found the first few days challenging.

Some pain, but not bad

Taking a shower—"tricky"

Jackie helps a lot

Still in uncharted territory, I needed to make a few initial adjustments—especially my sleeping arrangements. Still sore, I moved slowly and uncomfortably. It was difficult to lie down completely, but I could stretch out on our rocker/recliner chair. So that piece of furniture became my bed for several days.

Sleep in recliner

Protect wound from cat in bed

Soon be back with Ben

Although I felt impatient about regaining my strength and health, I reminded myself that healing was a process, and that I just needed to pay attention to my body and follow the doctor's instructions.

Slow, but progressing

Using breathing equipment

Helps strengthen my lungs

Several days passed, and Jackie returned home. I resumed sleeping in my own bed, and I felt encouraged by the progress I was making.

Thankfully, the worst was over...or so I thought.

Chapter 7

Chemotherapy
A Change in the Script

Even though my internal map for healing had not included a lobectomy for cancer, I recalled navigating similar landscapes earlier in my life. Based on two prior surgeries— a tonsillectomy at age 7 and a partial hysterectomy at age 30—I felt confident about my power of recuperation.

A week after I left the hospital, it was time to check in with my surgeon, and I made a follow-up appointment to get my final stitches removed.

Fortunately, Ben and I didn't have a long wait to see the doctor. Squeamish by nature, I was anxious to put this entire episode behind me. I told the doctor that I dreaded any tugging on the small bandages covering the incision and hearing the snipping sounds that would follow. He was sensitive to my needs and stopped a couple of times to allow me to relax into the process.

Hang in there, I told myself. Only a few more minutes...and all this will seem just like a bad dream.

The doctor used humor to distract me from any discomfort I was experiencing during this procedure. However, once he completed his task, his upbeat demeanor changed.

His eyes narrowed and his jaw tightened as he picked up a manilla folder from his desk. He read aloud from the report of the biopsy he had performed during my lung surgery. "...Out of the 24 lymph nodes removed, 6 lymph nodes **have been identified as positive for cancer.**" The doctor further, explained that I had Stage 2B Lung Cancer (Stage 4 being most severe), and that **chemotherapy** was the next course of treatment.

Sighing deeply, he handed me a sheet of paper with the name of an a respected oncologist, and suggested that I make an appointment with her as soon as possible.

Not another doctor! I have heard all those horror stories about chemo. Even the word **oncologist** *frightens me. Now I need to see one to treat me?*

Doctor appears sad

Recommends oncologist

More treatment needed

I had not anticipated this new information. It totally shattered any illusions I had about relinquishing my "patient" status in the near future.

No! No! This is NOT what I expected. I thought they got all the cancer when they removed the tumor and my left lobe!

Not even healed yet

Now take toxic chemicals

Can I handle this?

In an attempt to block the negative thoughts that were hijacking the microphone in my head, I started affirming *one moment at a time...one step at a time...one day at a time.*

I left the surgeon's office dazed, scared and resigned about what needed to happen next.

This illness—from which I thought I was recovering—had now tightened its grip on my life. As I headed deeper into the nightmarish landscape called cancer, I imagined a huge, red DETOUR sign blocking my path towards health.

NEW TERRITORY

Later that day, after I composed myself, I scheduled an appointment to meet with the newest member of my medical team, the oncologist.

Here we were again. Only this time, it was an oncologist's office where Ben and I waited.

The female doctor who greeted us was a smart, feisty,"take-no-prisoners" cancer fighter. She had been a warrior on this battlefield many times; and, later, she would prove to be a powerful advocate for getting tests results and insurance approvals handled quickly.

After examining my records, the doctor explained my condition and the requirements to begin treatment. She

77

spoke her instructions in rapid-fire English—spiced with a Romanian accent.

Meet oncologist

"To Do List", rapidly said

Overwhelming me

Once her litany began, my thoughts started swirling like errant clothes in my dryer's spin cycle.

"Get a calendar."

"Track appointments, blood counts, tests…"

"Get implant in chest!"

Oh no! Another surgery!

Dread, fear and repulsion filled me when I learned that a port-a-catheter implant would be needed. This device would be placed inside my chest and used as the injection site for administering the chemotherapy.

I am one of the few remaining people on the planet who has not gotten her ears pierced. It is not a fashion statement. I love earrings—I just hate needles and puncture holes even more. Just the thought of an implant made me woozy.

While I was still reeling from the necessity of having a port-a-catheter inserted into my chest, the doctor educated me about the two prescriptions of chemo that would be administered.

Side-effects explained

Feel the fear...and do it still

Keep moving forward...

The doctor's mouth kept moving, and I heard some additional "noises" that sounded like...

Expect to be bald

Medicine for vomiting

Body will react

Now she's talking about an entire list of things I need to avoid...I probably should tune in again...

My stomach tightened, and I flushed with anger as the oncologist's litany of "don'ts" continued to grow.

Don't eat raw foods now

Don't take anti-oxidants

Don't use a razor

Don't drink alcohol

Don't clean cat's litter boxes

Don't be in a crowd

Don't be around kids

Don't eat food without peeling

Don't, don't, don't, don't, don't!!!

Even as I was taking notes, I was fighting to keep my mind from shutting out her words.

Fortunately, Ben was here.

Holy cow! She's still talking...

When the consultation ended, I limply extended my hand to receive the two books about cancer that she suggested I read.

Can't handle all this

Leave office with head swimming

Too much to absorb

I felt as though I had just been swept up into the swiftly moving currents of a white water river, and all I could do was surrender.

Taking the Next Steps...

If I think about this too much, I might book passage to an undisclosed destination in South America.

Later that day, I called my VATS surgeon and scheduled an appointment for the port-a-catheter out-patient procedure. The day of the minor surgery came and went quickly. Several hours after being admitted to the hospital, I awoke in the recovery room—resting comfortably. Ben was notified that everything went smoothly, and, shortly, I would be ready to return home.

It really wasn't as bad as I had imagined—just some occasional, strange sensations afterwards.

Surgery complete

Implant in chest...scrapes inside

Outside protrusion

Okay...another completion check on my never-ending "To Do List".

There were more steps I needed to take before the actual chemotherapy session.

I needed to fill my two anti-nausea prescriptions at the pharmacy.

Before chemo starts...

Pills to prevent vomiting

(I hope they will work!)

With each completed task from my set of instructions, the anticipation of what I might be experiencing grew stronger.

Blood counts important...

Need to schedule them weekly

(Get used to needles!)

There's still more to remember...

Drink lots of water

Replenish at hospital

(If necessary)

All too soon my first chemotherapy session would begin. However, Ben and I did have some precious time for our pent up emotions to surface.

Hugging each other

Ben and I share tears and fears...

Gain some needed strength

Chapter 8

Preparing for the Next Part of the Journey
C-C-C...Courage

After I checked off several more tasks on my "To Do List", I wanted to exert control over those areas of my life where it was possible.

The hospital where I would be receiving my chemotherapy treatments offered a variety of free cancer support classes, and I decided to attend the ones I thought would be most helpful. Some included caregivers as well.

Meditation group

Ben and I reduce some stress

Go to painting class

Also, the American Cancer Society sponsors a great workshop called, **Look Good...Feel Better** to help women deal with the image changes they will be experiencing during treatment.

Look Good...Feel Better

Go to workshop on cancer

Skin care, wigs, makeup

Participating in these activities helped me feel less like the subject of a mad scientist's research project and more like the person I was before my diagnosis.

During a shopping mall walk, I made an impromptu and important decision. I looked for a beauty salon with a walk-in appointment policy, and I found one. I told the hair stylist that I would be undergoing chemotherapy and asked her to cut my shoulder length hair very short.

Under the blades of her razor-edged scissors and her compassionate precision, the beautician cut my hair into a short, sassy style. I looked in the mirror and then wistfully at the myriad pieces of tinted blonde hair that now covered the floor beneath me.

I turned my gaze back at the reflection in the glass. The woman who stared back at me looked familiar, but different. My face was framed more distinctively, and my natural, platinum roots were apparent now. I felt exposed and free at the same time.

Seeking more support

Classes for changes ahead

Bald? Choose to cut hair!

In this atmosphere of change, I felt certain of one thing—the person who emerged from the barber chair was becoming more authentic.   But before I could begin to fully embrace the *new* me, I would have to start with baby steps.

The haircut was a significant change, but I still clung to my old image.   If baldness was my future, I wanted a wig that would resemble my old hair style.

As a proactive measure, I made a date with Teena to go wig "shopping" at the hospital. At that time, there was a program for cancer patients to receive a free wig of their choice.

Rather than dwell on what I had been told would be my inevitable hair loss, I decided to make the "perfect-wig-hunt" a fun excursion.   With Teena's whole-hearted encouragement, I plopped a variety of wigs in various styles and colors on my head.   After a good laugh, I finally made a choice and brought my first wig home.

There were other helpful and empowering things I did before, during and after treatment:

- Daily outdoor walks exercised my body while Mother Nature nurtured my mind and spirit.

- I wrote a healing affirmation—a positive, present tense statement—on every index card of a small, spiral notebook. I read these words during my treatment sessions and at various times throughout the day.

Healing Affirmations
"Every day in every way I am getting better and better."

"The breath of life flows easily through me"

"I lovingly live life to the fullest."

Affirmations Before, During and After a Medical Procedure

"Every hand that touches me is a healing hand and expresses only love."

"I am comfortable at all times."

- Several clinical hypnosis friends offered support, and I asked them to record hypnosis CD's to alleviate nausea and other possible side-effects of chemotherapy.

- I recorded a CD, *Relax and Revitalize in Just 10 Minutes* which proved to be a useful tool for de-stressing. It contains a guided meditation for deep relaxation and a separate track of pre-recorded mind-body affirmations.

- Another mind-body tool—similar to hypnosis—is creative visualization. I also purchased a package of CD's, created for cancer patients, by guided imagery expert, Belleruth Naperstek.

- Ben and I both scheduled appointments with the oncology social worker at the hospital. She was a great navigational resource who helped us prepare for the journey ahead. Additionally, she proved to be a safe harbor where we could talk about our fear, anger and hope.

- When I learned that our social worker was also a trained Reiki Master (see below), I scheduled several sessions with her to receive the benefits of this gentle, yet powerful, energetic healing modality.

"The word Reiki is made of two Japanese words - Rei which means "God's Wisdom or the Higher Power" and Ki which is "life force energy". So Reiki is actually "spiritually guided life force energy."

A treatment feels like a wonderful glowing radiance that flows through and around you. Reiki treats the whole person including body, emotions, mind and spirit creating many beneficial effects that include relaxation and feelings of peace, security and wellbeing. Many have reported miraculous results." –Source www.Reiki.org

- Another healing technique I used is called Meridian Tapping (also known as EFT—emotional freedom technique) which is self-administered finger-tip tapping on certain acupressure meridians to help release emotional and physical distress.

The time for my first chemo treatment was fast approaching, and I was comforted by the mind/body "toolkit" I had assembled. Soon I would put all of them to use.

Chapter 9

Treatment Begins...
We Are Definitely Not in Kansas, Anymore

The day of my first chemotherapy session arrived, and I headed deeper into the unknown regions of Cancer Territory. My guides for this excursion were the hospital administrative staff, the nurses and volunteers at the Cancer Unit at the hospital.

When I entered the building that had the words, CANCER engraved above the doorway, I felt teary and reverent—like I had entered a holy place. The people I saw were here to "fight the good fight"— the scouts, the foot soldiers, wounded veterans, and those war weary officers who had been given their marching papers again. They were all WELLNESS WARRIORS, and I was about to join their ranks.

I stopped at the information desk, and I was given directions to the chemotherapy treatment area. As Ben and I headed down the corridor towards the small room where I would sit for the next eight hours, my fingers gripped his hand with a vice-like ferocity.

The room was cramped, and I did not expect to see two other people (in various stages of "combat") already hooked up to I.V. drips. I looked about the tight quarters and wished the space were larger and that the walls were painted a cheery color. A longing to see live, growing green plants (or at least pictures of them) overpowered me. The drabness of the chemo treatment surroundings only emphasized my feelings of heaviness and dread.

Three to a small room

Ominous I. V. poles loom

Two people are here

I was told that my personalized prescription was being prepared by a specially trained oncology pharmacist and that it would be ready shortly.

"Chemo being brewed...

Specially made just for you...

One is *metal*-based"

I broke the rules immediately when I asked if Ben could sit in the room with me. The area was so small that there was little space for the nurses to maneuver. Yet, the staff was understanding and recognized the need that was so strong for both of us—to be close and "normalize" this procedure.

Ben was allowed to sit with me. However, the nurses or another patient, could request him to leave.

If caregivers choose to stay for the duration of the treatment session, it is important for them take *breathers* and find their own comfortable space during this time. Everyone needs a break.

Not surprisingly, I was given more instructions about the treatment and handed additional information about chemotherapy. I was grateful that I had Ben nearby to help me absorb it.

Given things to read

Info parsed in small doses

More will be coming

This is really going to happen! Oh no! Not a word from the governor's office? No reprieve? Fear of the unknown—my worst enemy—was playing out overly dramatic scenarios in my head.

Sheesh! This is taking forever...let's get on with it.

The time has come...NOW

Hooked up to stand beside me

Bags of clear liquid

The first treatment was the most important time for emotional "hand-holding". Looking at the face of my beloved was comforting and reassuring—and as I mentioned earlier—pain-reducing.

The only pain I felt, however, was the prick of the I.V. line as it entered my port-a-catheter. For a needle-aversion gal, this was a piece of cake.

Needle in my port

Fluids contain platinum

Life more prized than gold

The day that stretched before me seemed to have no horizon.

Chemo in body

Drip-by-drip—process is slow

Six to eight hours left

To help pass the time and to become informed about the type of chemo being administered and its possible side effects, I was given another set of photocopied papers.

More pages to read

Nurse reviews information

Reveals side-effects

As part of my *own* treatment plan, I had packed a bag containing a homemade lunch, my series of hand-written affirmations, a copy of my own recording of *Relax and Revitalize in Just 10 Minutes CD,* several other hypnosis CD's that my skilled and supportive colleagues had recorded for me—as well as—the creative visualization CD's by Belleruth Naperstek.

Time to hear CD's

Listen to hypnosis now

Close eyes—leave this place

After placing the earphones on my head that were attached to my portable CD player, I shut my eyes, took a few cleansing breaths, and enjoyed a nice respite from all the outer activity.

It was comforting having people checking on me—not only the nursing staff—but those incredibly thoughtful and generous unpaid helpers, the volunteers. Their sweet and cheerful demeanors provided a calming balm during this lengthy procedure.

Thoughtful Volunteers

Bring compassion...pillows...food

Everyone is kind

There were several three-person treatment rooms adjacent to one another with only a heavy duty curtain separating us, so it was easy to overhear conversations and activity from the "other side".

A short time after I was hooked up, I heard some voices, followed by disturbing sounds.

Stirrings next to me...

Paramedics called to help

Man leaves on stretcher

While I assured myself that this was not the norm (which is true), it did unnerve me a bit.

Reassuring? Not!

Next set of pages given

Still, there's more to read

Chemo continues...

Eat something...sleep some

One bag of chemo empty

Taking forever!

When my machine began to beep, I was ecstatic because it signaled the end of first bag of medicine. As I had been told, a second smaller bag of liquids comprising a different chemical mixture was now attached to my I. V. pole.

There was something else I hadn't anticipated. With all this liquid going in, some also needed to go out. I had to pee...but I required assistance.

I rang the buzzer to summon a nurse to help ease me out of the chair. I had been sitting with my feet elevated on the recliner's extended foot rest—which was great for sleeping, but not for movement. (No pun intended).

Once I was mobile, Ben who had resumed his vigil, made sure he escorted me to the restroom and waited patiently to help me back to my room.

Need a bathroom break

Push the I.V. stand with me

Feel the needle tug

I admit it was a bit tricky the first time, but by the time I had visited the bathroom about 3-4 times, I had the hang of it and avoided any pulling on the needle.

The day continued to drag, but after about two more hours I heard the now familiar auditory alert.

Machine starts to beep

Sounds signal *End of Round One*

Three MORE treatments left

Relieved and a bit tired, Ben and I packed up my "goodie" bag. I was more than ready to return to the familiar surroundings of home.

However, I was given one more of set of instructions.

Would they never end?

Flush toilet two times

Keep Ben safe from chemicals

Oh my...toxic dump!

Not knowing what to expect after returning home, I was happy and surprised to feel hungry.

Home now, eat dinner

Symptoms...just feel *different*

What will body do?

I have learned through my own journey, that everyone's experience with various treatments and chemo is different. While having read about the "possible" side-effects of my chemical brew was helpful, I knew that words were powerful.

I was hopeful that what I read was only descriptive and not prescriptive of what would follow.

During dinner, I did have some expected reactions.

Smells more intense now

Metallic taste in my mouth

Food tastes different

I got through that night and the next 48 hours with just olfactory changes and a tinny flavor that lingered in my mouth.

The anxiety of "What's next?" would intermittently break into my thoughts like a burglar intent on stealing my sanity.

Few days pass...they're calm

Feel tired and uneasy

But NO VOMITING!

I had been advised to "stay ahead" of the nausea. This meant taking a mild anti-nausea medication at the first symptom of queasiness. I also had a stronger anti-nausea medication that I could take if I felt worse.

That was good advice, and I followed it.

Determined to maintain as much normalcy as possible, I confirmed a previously scheduled meeting with a Medicare insurance broker. Since I was a new enrollee in the program, I needed information about my medical benefits and financial responsibilities.

It was one more tedious appointment on my "To Do" calendar. Perhaps, it was that attitude that influenced what happened next.

Sitting next to Ben in a small, stuffy room, I squinted at the sheets of numerical tables that the insurance agent had placed on the desk in front of us. Suddenly, I felt extremely nauseous. I abruptly jumped out of my chair, sputtering, "I am going to vomit!" Ben sprang to *his* feet.

I can still see our Medicare advisor's frozen, open jawed face as he watched us **both** sprint towards the **Ladies' Room.**

After bursting through the bathroom door, I began retching. While Ben held my head and shoulders, the meager contents of my stomach exploded into the first available toilet bowl.

Can't continue here

Need to leave and reschedule

Meeting is on "hold"

It is amazing how vomitting alters your priorities...

Will I Always Feel Like This?

Despite drinking water and other liquids to replenish the fluids I had lost during my vomiting "episodes" and despite the two medications I was taking to curb queasiness, I felt terrible.

The last thing I wanted to do was return to the Day Hospital, but I couldn't avoid it any longer. I needed a rehydration treatment.

Call doctor's office

Schedule rehydration

Receive infusion

111

Back in dreary room

Hours attached to I.V. drip

Makes me feel better

It took two more treatments, but by the end of the third day of treatment I was a completely different person than the one who had entered several days earlier.

Two more days…get drip

Know this helps, but don't like it

Each day, feel better

I was overwhelmed by the amount of information I was tracking. Additionally, I felt "fuzzy-minded" (difficulty focusing, concentrating and remembering). For those of us

112

in a certain age bracket, think of it as "senior moments" on steroids.

This condition has a medical name: Chemo Brain.

The Beat Goes On... And You Learn to Dance

Thankfully, on the advice of my oncologist, I had purchased a 3-ring binder to keep my medical records, test results and appointment calendar in one place.

My life and Ben's now revolved around medical appointments.

One week get chemo

Two weeks to get my blood counts

Third week MORE chemo

See oncologist

Discuss tests and new symptoms

Regular visits

The question that often came to mind was: "How do I feel today?" That thought usually gave rise to fear and anxiety, but it also gave me the opportunity to pay more attention to my body messages and to honor them.

Seek a "normal" day

Room, people, food odors strong!

Taste buds...unfriendly

Although I wished I could have pushed a magical PAUSE button, daily life and its demands didn't stop during the chemo regime and its challenges.

Routine chores provided a semblance of my life before cancer and helped me focus on what I **could** do each day.

Do the things I can

Diminished activities

Longing for "healthy"

Some days, though, these tasks felt crushing.

Pay bills, do laundry

Buy groceries, cook the meals

Pick up prescriptions

115

I can't imagine handling all of these stressors alone. Unfortunately, some people living with cancer struggle every day without the additional emotional and physical help they need.

I was one of the lucky ones. My dear husband—who continued to work full time during my entire journey back to health—steadfastly, and uncomplainingly, took care of me and walked each step with me on my path to wellness.

Ben, family, friends, medical personnel and volunteers supported and uplifted me during those most challenging times. In her song, *I am Gonna Love You Through It,* Martina McBride poignantly captures the healing that comes from being surround by love.

Gifts...calls...notes arrive

So much love surrounds me now

Surprises comfort

Savor the small joys

Daily gratitude focus

Creates deep meaning

My sense of time changed during this treatment period. Some days felt excruciatingly slow. Those were times I described on my phone chats with Teena as not feeling my "perky" self.

Other times, the days whizzed past me signalling the arrival of my next chemotherapy session.

117

Follow schedule

Get chemo...(three-week cycle)

Rebound for two weeks

It was **that** time again.

Just when feeling good...

It's time again for treatment.

Fear...but keep going!

It helped to think about having **one session already behind me**.

I did it, and I could do it again...was my rallying call.

Think what's accomplished

Only three more rounds to go

Bolsters my spirit

Sitting in a small room with two other people of different ages, in various stages of their illness, who were also receiving treatment gave me strength to be a Wellness Warrior, too.

"Can do" attitude

Important: stay positive

Feel Ben's love...hold hands

The second round of chemo was fairly routine. At least I knew what to expect. The nausea hit about 48 hours after my treatment. I did vomit again, but it wasn't severe. However, I did require rehydration again, but unlike the first time, it was only for one day.

I rebounded for two weeks and scheduled my next treatment.

When my third session loomed close, I decided to bring some much-needed levity into the somber surroundings of the chemo room. So, I decided to costume myself for the part of prankster.

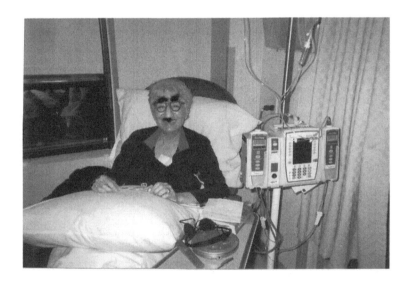

Close to Halloween

Fake nose, glasses for chemo

Laughter helps treatment

I so enjoyed letting my rambunctious, joyful Inner Child play—a part of myself that still felt like *me*.

Waiting for the arrival of unsuspecting patients, volunteers and the nursing staff made my treatment time go much faster. I loved seeing their eyes widen with surprise and hearing giggles become deep-throated laughter .

The next two weeks passed fairly quickly.

Then it was time again for my next round of blood tests, and, gratefully, my LAST chemotherapy session.

I prepared myself mentally, emotionally and physically as best I could. I made sure Ben and I had a camera to record this momentous occasion, and that we were both in the picture. I wrote down the words in big bold letters, **MY LAST CHEMO**, on a sheet of notebook paper to announce my upgraded status. I made sure it was in plain sight. If someone did not notice, I told them.

When I left the chemo treatment area that day, I raised my arm and turned my wrist mimicking the gesture used by the Queen of England when addressing her loyal subjects.

Everyone within earshot heard my announcement: **"I finished chemo today**!"

Despite the knowledge that I would soon endure the the crappy side-effects (pun intended) of my healing elixirs, I turned exurberantly towards the exit.

Can do this...once more!

Bring sign: LAST CHEMO TODAY

Leave waving midst cheers

It Didn't Come to Stay...It Came to Pass

Finally, it was over!

Two more weeks passed, and I had endured. I was ready to reclaim some normalcy, again.

At my follow-up appointment with my oncologist, she matter-of-factly wrote down some of the familiar side effects from my last—and final--treatment. As her pen moved back and forth across the page of notes, she did not register any concerns. Then she cocked her head to one side and muttered. "She did not lose her hair!"

This result was completely unanticipated—especially since she had written a prescription for a wig at our first meeting. Feeling the top of my head and stroking my short, nearly completely platinum white hair, I grinned my best Mona Lisa smile.

Check in with doctor

State symptoms from last chemo

She writes: *"Still has hair!"*

Reminiscing About the Journey...

Without warning, I was catapulted back in time. Just like one of those movie flashback scenes, I saw myself in my oncologist's office recalling the certainty in her voice as she predicted the outcome from my two chemo mixtures, plus the two prescribed anti-nausea medications—all of them stating baldness as their side-effect.

"I'll write you a prescription for a wig," she said.

125

Hair…there…everywhere…

Pronouncement: "You will be bald!"

Expect new image

"No!" I silently screamed. Cancer has already taken part of my lung, what else does it want from me?

After the anger and sadness subsided, I decided to prepare for the inevitable—**complete hair loss.**

The movie in my head back flashed back in time to a different scene (mentioned earlier in the book) when I attended the Amercian Cancer Society's workshop, **Look Good, Feel Better.** This class is designed to help women who are undergoing cancer treatment adjust to alterations in their physical appearance.

Prepare for changes

Go to makeup, wig tips class

For *cancer* patients

I remember being flooded with a mixture of emotions when I entered the classroom. The immediate gratitude I felt for the **volunteer** hair-skin-nail specialist, who greeted us, turned into resentment.

*She is so pretty, energetic...all the things I am **not**.. How dare she flaunt her health!*

As I looked around the room at the other women, my resentment was replaced by fear and dread.

127

Bald women are here

Is this what *I* will look like

Despite beauty tips?

I watched as these women, my courageous sister travelers—several weak and scarred from the journey—gathered around the large table laden with cosmetics, scarves and wigs, and took their seats.

Tears of admiration filled my eyes as I allowed my sister patients' warrior spirit to wash over me.

We are NOT our hair

Whether here or barely there

Something GREAT shines though

It has been said that a woman's **hair** is her crowning glory. But in that room on that day, it was clear that a woman's **eyes**—the windows to her soul—reflected her unfathomable inner beauty.

See deep into eyes

For some lashes...brows...missing

Soul NOT affected

With some direction and guidance from our instructor, we each put on foundation to make our faces glow again, used eye brow pencil to draw and to color the place where brows and lashes had once existed, and tied colorful scarves in various configurations to give the illusion of hair beneath. One women tried on a hat with hair on either side and another modeled a full wig.

Look good, feel better

Be empowered, "Yes we can"

See and then believe

My reverie of these past events vanished as quickly as they had started, and my thoughts returned to my oncologist's office.

The doctor, who always seemed to have an explanation for everything, was now completing her notes and still muttering under her breath bewilderment over my intact head of hair.

I can only conjecture that the use of complementary healing tools such as Reiki, affirmations, a positive attitude, humor, guided imagery and hypnosis CD's eased my discomfort, and also helped me keep my hair.

Cancer War declared

Hair is Resistance Fighter

Refuses to leave!

My physical appearance **did change**, however, during the course of my journey. Inside the cover of my 3-ring Medical Book Binder (where I kept all my test results, medications, doctors appointments and other important documentation) I placed a picture of myself **before** the cancer diagnosis. The photo showed me sporting a navy blue workout suit and shoulder length highlighted blonde hair. I wrote on the top of the page "Marjorie's Vibrant Health Book." I also surrounded the picture with a photo of myself as a strong, fun-loving two-year old and another picture of myself from my website that reminded me of activity and contribution.

These were the images I held in my mind throughout treatment and the pictures I saw every time I needed to refer to my medical information.

These powerful images sustained me, but I couldn't deny that I was physically changing. I had already cut my hair—in anticipation of becoming bald—and each week I saw my blonde-tinted hair color slowly receding into just the tips of my remaining hair.

Each week exposed more of the color that I had been covering up at the hair salon in order to avoid looking older. My roots were white! My hair stylist described it more artistically and kindly as *Platinum.*

Ironically, my chemo mixture actually contained the metal, *platinum*, that was supposed to contribute to my hair loss.

Battles with chemo

"Platinum" ingredient

Becomes hair color

Day after day, the mirror was reflecting someone I didn't quite recognize or know very well, yet.

New image appears...

What remains is Authentic

The dyed blonde is gone

It took time to embrace the "new" me, but she helped me discover the parts of myself that needed to be reclaimed and those previously disowned.

Hair...victorious!

Chemo changed by alchemy

Into the Real Me

As a tribute to my Emerging Self, I added an additional picture to my Medical Book Binder Cover that I now fondly call the Platinum Kid.

Ah, but I am getting ahead of myself...because chemo was NOT the end of my treatment and the use of my Medical Book Binder.

Chapter 10

Radiation
Where Are My Ruby Slippers?

At my next appointment with the oncologist, she pored over my reports. Looking up from the paperwork, she explained that because 6 of the 24 lymph nodes that had been biopsied during my lobectomy had tested positive for cancer, radiation was my best option for **complete** remission.

Triumphant, but physically and mentally exhausted from my chemotherapy sessions, I thought about the pros and cons of subjecting my body to yet another medical intervention.

Just the mention of scheduling another set of appointments with *another* doctor with *another* title with *another* set of rules threatened to send me running from the room screaming, "**No Way!**"

Once I was semi-rational again, I realized that the best course of action was to discuss it with my doctor, research the options, listen to my intuition and, finally, make the *best* choice based on the *best* information I gathered.

Sometimes, you have the luxury of taking your time in exploring options in your life—like selecting a paint color for the living room. Unfortunately, certain medical decisions require a much quicker response.

While it is true that most procedures, medicines and treatments do have *possible* side effects, I needed to remember that every person's physical makeup is unique, and that it would be impossible to predict how *my* body would behave.

I had endured surgery and chemo. Now there was just one intervention left to annihilate any remaining cancer cells—radiation.

Overcoming my initial reluctance, I said, "Okay, let's begin radiation."

The Treatment Procedure

Due to the effects of chemo brain, I was already experiencing fuzzy-headedness and difficulty concentrating. When I called to make my first appointment to begin treatment, I learned there were several other appointments that needed to be made, but they were given to me without clarifying the specific order in which I needed to proceed.

Next steps not explained

Need to be own advocate

Stress and frustration!!

Even making a simple phone call during that time seemed to suck up inordinate amounts of energy. Scheduling the next series of appointments and another CT scan was one of those energy vacuums. I found myself in a round of phone trees, leaving messages and waiting for someone to call me back.

When I was able to contact a real person, I received confusing information about the sequence of the required appointments before we could begin treatment. It was getting close to the Thanksgiving and Christmas Holiday season and scheduling would become even more complicated.

Treatment is delayed

CT...then simulation

Why wasn't I told?

Anger gripped my thoughts. *Why doesn't the scheduler have a written copy of the procedures and their sequenced appointments to give to the patient?*

In the privacy of my home, I yelled all the profanity I could remember (even making up some new ones) at all the real and imaginary incompetent people who were giving me the confusing information.

A "people pleaser" for most of my life, confrontations make me very uncomfortable. However, suppressing my anger was an unhealthy choice. Re-directed anger, however, could lead to inspired action—and maybe even create positive change—especially for other new patients.

Once I had exhausted my anger—and nearly my voice—I decided that I could now speak calmly and rationally on the phone to the hospital's scheduling department. I relayed my frustration and upset in having my treatment delayed by misinformation—as well as—ideas for preventing other patients from having to add this unnecessary stress to their already full plates.

I assured the woman with whom I spoke that I wanted to be helpful and reduce the work for *everyone* involved. She listened attentively and offered her apologies. Then she carefully and clearly listed the appointments that needed to be made and the precise order.

Call the scheduler...

Share concerns and solutions

Stand in my power

When I hung up the phone, I was feeling better both emotionally and physically.

The next day I was surprised when the radiologist, to whom I had been referred (but had not as yet met), called *personally* to address the problems I had encountered. He promised that the issues would be rectified.

Phone call reassures

Apologies for the stress

Let's begin again

I already liked this doctor.

Ben and I met with the oncology radiologist, a kindly, soft-spoken, young Asian doctor, who thoroughly informed us about radiation and the possible side-effects.

Consultation first

Create "map" for laser beam

Discuss side-effects

Hard time swallowing?

Difficulty with breathing?

Burns? All possible?

Yikes! I had just finished chemo. Do I really want to do this? Would there be no end to this whirlwind of decision-making?

Reminded myself

I am not a statistic

Decide to do it...

The next appointment consisted of identifying and mapping precisely, and strategically, the exact locations to focus the radiation beam.

Simulation next

Draw blue target marks on chest

"Tattoos" stay on skin

Now that I was properly prepped, I scheduled my first radiation treatment.

I arrived (with Ben, of course) at the Radiation Building at the hospital...wondering how *this* experience would unfold.

The door to the radiation room opened and a nurse, holding my chart , called my name. Stepping inside with her,   I waved a shakey "goodbye" to Ben. Then she led me to a sign-in area—explaining that I would report here five days a week for five and one-half weeks.

Instructions given

Mondays...sign-in, then weigh-in

Put on gown and wait

Once inside the Women's Dressing Room, I undressed and put on the all-too familiar hospital gown. I sat down in the waiting area and watched a series of women entering and leaving. I began chatting nervously with the two women who were sitting in the chairs beside me, also waiting to be called for treatment.

"This is my first time," I said to the entire room of women (and no one in particular) hoping to get the reassurance I so desperately needed. Thankfully, my sister sojourners offered comforting words and reassuring smiles.

Then I heard a phantom voice announce: "Marjorie Miles."

Loud speaker calls name

"We are ready for you now."

Walk into chamber

A female technician greeted me, and I followed her down the corridor.

Since there were no locks for the lockers in the dressing room, I remember thinking how funny I must have appeared during my walk—wearing an oversized hospital gown and a shoulder-strap purse.   When stressed my thoughts to fashion.

Lie down on table

Machine moves beam back and forth

It's over quickly

I was surprised how fast the treatment was. It took less time for the radiation procedure than it did to get undressed and dressed again. It was not invasive or uncomfortable.

Whew! What a relief.

I was scheduled for daily visits Mondays through Fridays at 10:00 AM for 5 ½ weeks. Ben drove me to the appointments. However, after two weeks of treatment, we were both convinced that I was handling the radiation well. So I decided to drive myself to the hospital for the remaining sessions.

Any activity or task that I could assume (or resume) added to my sense of well being, so I happily went to the appointments alone.

This is my "job" now

Breakfast...then radiation

Drive to appointment

I developed a routine and made sure I listened to my body. Fatigue was something I needed to honor, but usually I had enough energy to have lunch with Teena once a week—another restorative activity for mind-body-spirit.

149

Mornings are best time

Rest of day belongs to me

Errands, lunch, and rest

During treatment, I had a weekly appointment with the radiologist to review my body's reactions and to ask questions. Basically, I was just experiencing fatigue.

Will symptoms increase?

Talk with the doctor weekly

Side effects questioned

I was doing fine, except for the anxiety of being in unknown territory again.

Relief after zap

Count the sessions completed

So far, I'm okay

Then I had a couple of symptoms that were new to me. A cough started that week, along with some tightness and discomfort in my chest. So at my next Monday visit, I shared these changes with the radiologist who was covering my regular doctor's appointments that day.   Because these symptoms were minimal, I debated mentioning them. This doctor, however, thought differently. He wanted to rule out a possible pulmonary embolism and told me to go straight to the Emergency Room. I thought he was overreacting to my symptoms, but he was insistent.

A cough, tightness, pain

Not bad, but doctor concerned

Visit to the ER

Notoriously directionally-challenged, I was more concerned about how I would navigate the huge hospital campus from my current location to the Emergency Room than I was about my health risk. Luckily, my favorite nurse overheard the conversation, knew a shortcut and volunteered to walk with me to my destination.

I phoned Ben about my new situation, and he arrived within the hour only to find me still sitting in the overcrowded ER lobby. It seemed that everyone else that day decided to have their own emergency.

Once I was admitted, the ER doctor ordered a heart monitor, a chest x-ray and another CT scan.

Ben here with me now

X-Ray, CT scan again

Wear heart monitor

Fortunately, I was not experiencing a pulmonary embolism— a life threatening condition. Instead, the test results showed a relatively common issue, pulomonary effusion, fluid buildup around the lungs—a condition that usually diminishes and heals on its own.

Fluid around lung

Address, if symptoms increase

Back to old routine

153

88
8

While no one wants to go the Emergency Room, The ER physician gave Ben and me some unexpected good news. My heart was strong and in reviewing both the X-ray and the CT scan, he could find no evidence of cancer!

The following day, I returned confidently for my next radiation treatment.

Images From Another Time...

About a week later, while I was sitting in the Women's Dressing Room waiting for my name to be called, I glanced around the room at the other patients. My mind drifted, and my thoughts flashed to another, darker experience in human history—The Holocaust.

Those thoughts then became words that flowed out in a stream of consciousness series of three haiku:

We all have "tattoos"

Bald, short hair, some hair grown back

Same hospital gowns

Images flash by

"Concentration Camp Women"

Waiting to be *called*

Names heard on speaker

Each leaves—lead into chamber

What about *her* fate?

Just as quickly as those negative images had appeared, new pictures and thoughts replaced them. I was in a healing place—not a death camp—and I was surrounded by courageous sister-patients, who even in a weakened physical state, exuded a special strength that comes from a courageous warrior's heart.

This new vision filled me with inspiration, optimism and hope.

Death gets no voice here

Sharing hope, support...courage

We are *survivors!*

Kindness, compassion

This experience bonds us

Strangers united

Meeting My Poetry Muse

The weeks passed and I continued my daily treatments. Everything seemed fairly routine now, including my pre-scheduled appointments every Wednesday to meet with my radiologist.

At one of those Wednesday appointments—for which I don't have a specific date—my life changed forever.

That was the day I heard the "Voice"...and the first haiku arrived in my radiologist's office.

The following day, I began my first haiku journal. I purchased a notebook and began writing three haiku every morning to reflect upon and integrate what had occurred since my cancer diagnosis—as well as—what was currently unfolding each day.

157

New angle now used

New symptoms felt in body

Five sessions remain

Regardless of what was happening to my body, I learned from illness that I was more than any physical suffering or my fears. I discovered that there is something in each of us that is luminous and magical and remains untouched by disease. It is transcendent—and poetry is its voice. To hear that voice is to know what healing means. It is a return to wholeness.

Close to the Finish Line

I was nearing the end of my 5 ½ weeks of radiation. Soon the last part of all the cancer treatments I had endured would be over.

However, just as I was heading for the door to go to my final Friday appointment, the phone rang. When I answered, a caller from the hospital informed me that my treatment had been postponed. A perfunctory female voice announced, "The radiation machine is down, and it won't be repaired until Monday. All appointments for today are cancelled."

There were two machines at the hospital that were constantly in use. There were approximately 100 women (and men) receiving radiation on a daily basis, so it was not uncommon for the equipment to break down. It had happened twice before, but it wasn't *my* machine. Today it was.

Last day of fifth week

Phone rings...the machine is down

No treatment today

Dammit! I am so close. Now I have to add an additional day of treatment to next week. I wish this whole thing were over!

The reality that all treatment was coming to an end both buoyed my spirits and frightened me.

One more treatment left

Daily "medicine" ending

Mixed feelings expressed

Chapter 11

Crossing the Finishing Line
The Emerald City...At Last

On February 5, 2011 I walked into the Radiation Chamber for the very last time.

When I re-entered the Woman's Dressing Room after my final treatment, I shed the hospital gown quickly.   Dressed in my street clothes, I stepped out from behind the changing room door and proclaimed my new status to everyone within earshot: **"I had my last radiation session today!"**

Smiling patients and knowing staff applauded vigorously. Taking a few moments to really look at the women here, I realized that I would probably never see any of them again.

Made new connections

Powerful experience

A special "knowing"

In anticipation of this momentous occasion, I brought ten of my *"Relax and Revitalize in Just Ten Minutes"* CD's as a parting gesture to relieve the stress of those who were still in treatment and for those who administered it.

Share self with others

Take CD's to give as gifts

Give thanks for support

As I handed each person their gift, emotions gripped at my throat as I choked out each "goodbye". I would miss seeing my fellow travelers and the medical staff, but I was filled with hope and the anticipation of walking a new path: The Road to Wellness.

End "active" treatment

No medical staff checking

'Bye, sister patients

Gratefully, I accepted my certificate of completion and laughed. The official looking document—which the staff had created—displayed my name in bold print, followed by the letters Ph.D., defined as **Phinally Done**.

Relief---survived this!

Body no longer lasered

But "remedy" stops

Certain dates become inscribed in your consciousness. One was my cancer diagnois on June 16, 2010, another was my lobectomy surgery on July 28, 2010 .

On February 5, 2011, I added the date my radiation treatments ended.

As though a beautiful crown had been placed upon my head, I accepted my new title.

I was no longer a cancer patient, but **a cancer survivor!**

Chapter 12

Celebration!
There's No Place Like Home

It was midday when Ben and I left the grey radiation oncology building—shaking off any clinging remnants of the arduous cancer journey we had endured—and into the bright sunshine of a fresh California day.

It was time for celebration!

Feeling simultaneously exhausted and exhilarated, we drove to a lovely nearby restaurant to savor the flavors of victory, recount the story of our trek and revel in our myriad blessings.

Have lunch with husband

Make toast with a glass of wine

Reclaim things denied

Ben and I marveled at each of the divinely-orchestrated events that had occurred on the road from illness to healing. Joyful tears filled our eyes as we raised our glasses in tribute to all the people—from the medical community to family, friends, volunteers and patients—who were sojourners, supporters, and helpers on the road we had traveled.

Even on the loneliness part of the path, I remembered that others had walked these dark places before me...and survived.

Eight-month adventure

Body has endured all things

With Amazing Grace

The Divine Refrain

During my sleep that night, I heard the *The Voice again.* This time it was whispering a phrase over and over, *"Praise for My Body!"*...until it almost sounded like an old-time preacher sermonizing to his flock.

When I awoke in the morning, these haiku arrived:

Praise for My Body!

Eight-month "removal"

Gets cancer out of body...

Kills bad AND good cells

Praise for My Body!

Cut, chemo, lasers—

Harsh invaders used to heal

Knocked down...but not OUT

Praise for My Body!

Plant my body's Flag

Not wavering, but waving

Gratefully...PROUDLY

Praise for My Body!

Tears of joy flow free

Releasing all the dis-ease

Spirit Temple STANDS!

Honoring the Place Where Dreams, Poetry and Creative Expression Come to Life

Since the deepest meaning of any experience is carried by the unconscious mind, it makes sense that the first encounter with my disowned Poetry Muse came through a daydream and commented on my cancer experience. As a professional dream-worker, I value the creativity, wisdom and intuitive guidance that flow from sleep dreams and daydreams. Dreams and poetry—speaking—the same language of symbols, metaphors and archetypes—can help you hear meaning in illness and in all the events of your life—often for the first time.

Writing something down on paper makes the experience and feelings real. More importantly, it allows your emotions to become more manageable.

In the process of weaving together the story of what is happening, you are also weaving yourself back into wholeness. As I learned from reading my haiku journals, writing makes your experience "reviewable". Over time, you can see all the interwoven threads from this journey and each of your challenges as only a chapter in a larger story.

Writing, reading and reciting poems is a way of seeing and naming where you have been, where you are, and where you are going in life. When you write haiku, your intuitive guidance reveals **what you did not know you knew** before you wrote or read your own poetry. This moment of surprising yourself with your own words of wisdom—or of being surprised by the wisdom contained within others' poems—is at the heart of poetic healing.

If writing feels overwhelming at this time, try *reading* poetry. Reading poetry can be a great comfort and plant seeds for your own writing, later. According to researchers, poetry's hypnotic rhythm, flow, and imagery have a dramatic calming effect on the heart and your entire system.

While on the cancer journey, I retrieved my love of writing.

After my recovery, I discovered my passion for igniting the Creative Muse in others.

At that time, I received another directive from *The Voice*. This time I heard, "You need to start an expressive writing group."

This idea sounds like "get a band together, and you will be the tuba player."

However, over time, I've learned to stop myself from questioning this Inner Guide. Instead, I daydream. That's when the "magic" happens. An idea for using a waking dream meditation as a writing prompt and blending dream work—as so many creative artists have done in the past—popped into my head. Eventually, I formed the *Writing with Your Inner Dream Muse* group to help others find their own voices, too. This group of both beginning and advanced writers continues to thrive. And out of the cacophony of life's ups and downs, I am honored to hear the most beautiful heart songs.

Dear Reader, may you discover a deeper meaning from your experiences with (or without) cancer. And when you hear the creative calling of your own Authentic voice, I encourage *you t*o pick up a pen and express it.

The Journey Continues...

What remains is LOVE

Love body, family, friends

Thankful for each gift!

According to the ancient philospher, Heraclitus, you cannot step into into the same river twice. The river is changing and so are you. Life is constantly providing you with brand new experiences. I am not the same person today that I was before my cancer diagnosis. But rather than trying to recapture the past, I aspire to live in each creative, juicy moment that is here now. When I am centered in the present, I can flow freely in the river of life—allowing its current to take me downstream where I can merge with Ocean.

"Marjorie Miles, the Artist, Can Fly"
Drawn by Artist Marjorie Scheer and Sister Cancer Survivor

Epilogue

Picture Perfect
Written by Ben Miles

Picture perfect...

Who would know

About the sickness that laid you low?

And so you're back

Appetite and all...

Now it's Spring

We've survived the fall

Thank You... for reading *Healing Haikus—A Poetic Prescription for Surviving Cancer*.

I hope you enjoyed it. If you did, please help others readers find this book.

1. Write a review

2. *Like* my Facebook page

   https://www.facebook.com/pages/Healing-Haikus/402423169887237

3. Sign up for my new releases by email by contacting me at

   drmarjorie@journeyofyourdreams.com

   so you can find about the next book as soon as it is available.

About the Author

Marjorie Miles, DCH, MFT, a former psychology professor and psychotherapist, earned her doctorate in clinical hypnotherapy.

Dr. Marjorie has been interviewed on the radio and has appeared on television and film. A dream expert, she is featured, with director Wes Craven, in the documentary movie *Night Terrors*.

After the events of 911, she was a consultant for three years on the National Nightmare Hotline.

A gifted teacher, she is also listed in "Who's Who Among America's Teachers.

Dr. Marjorie fulfills her passion for creative expression as a Dream and Creativity Coach, a writer, poet, spoken word artist, and workshop presenter. Additionally, she facilitates a bi-weekly writer's group, *Writing with Your Inner Dream Muse* and offers workshops, and individual telephone dream interpretation sessions.

She lives with her husband and two quirky cats in Huntington Beach, CA
drmarjorie@journeyofyourdreams.com

Acknowledgments

There are so many people to whom I feel grateful—too numerous the mention here—but who are held in my heart. I apologize for any oversights.

Many thanks to all the doctors, hospital staff, volunteers and healers who put me back on the path to health. I am especially grateful to Dr. Richard Fischel, Dr. Peter Chen, and Dr. Andreea Nanci (and her supportive staff—especially Christine and Jovan), Lillian Reed, R.N., Nandini Narayanan, LCSW, Leticia Montiel, DCH, for her in-person hypnosis recordings, (and all my hypnosis colleagues for the healing scripts they submitted to me), Donna Kannard, Ph.D. (and all the participants in her EFT Tapping Group)

My sister-in-law, Jackie Savage, who provided loving home care, at a time when I needed it most.

All the Wellness Warriors I met on my journey, and, particularly Marjorie Scheer, sister cancer survivor and artist, who "saw" me whole—even before I did.

My loving friends and their gifts—both tangible and intangible—including Debbie Hart and Ron Masa, Ph.D., John Michael Dickinson (cancer survivor) and Carol Basile for their beautiful and spiritual art pieces), Rhonda De Jaynes, Jane Lake, DCH, Margaret Varga (and her entire family), and April Louis, D.Min.

Teena Armstrong, Ph.D., for over 27 years of friendship, for being a perennial presence in all my life "adventures", and one of the beta readers for this book.

To my other beta readers, Lillian Nader, Paula Marshall, Ben Miles, Ed.D., for your precious time, encouragement, and valuable feedback, and Heather S. Friedman Rivera, R.N., J.D. Ph.D. who—while working full-time and writing her own first fiction novel, *Quiet Water*—made time to read *my* manuscript.

 The talented people in my *Writing with Your Dream Muse* group--including Frances Pullin, Rebecca Proud, Liv Haugland, Angela Romee, Sharon Willett, Jorge Gavino and all the other participants who have shared their "voices" with me.

Kerri Draper, a sister cancer survivor, teacher and gifted healer. Thank you for your Reiki practice and your Project Reiki Free 4 Cancer.

For creative inspiration and loving support, Judy Ranieri-- who made my special pith helmet--and Mary Jane Blackwell, sister cancer survivor, who helped me imagine the first book cover design and the photographer for my back cover and About the Author Page.

To Jean Noel Bassoir for her professional assessment and suggestions for this book.

There aren't any words to express the gratitude for my family's love and support. Mom, my life-long cheerleader and Dad's "go for your dreams" spirit, my brother, Bill Meyer, and my cousin, Lynn Slivka, for their steadfast involvement, phone calls, presents, encouragement, and compassionate listening—and to their spouses, Gale Meyer and Barry Slivka, and all the other family members who shared their prayers and good wishes.

My dear Dr. John DeWitt for his ongoing chiropractic care, deep concern for my well-being and his insistence on a X-ray that uncovered a malignant growth that could have claimed my life.

For my husband Ben, soul mate and best friend, who lovingly assumed the role of caregiver, medical advocate and sojourner, I give thanks daily for your presence in my life.

Cover design by Laura Gordon
Photography by Mary Jane Blackwell
Website Israel Martinez Zelaya

Made in the USA
Middletown, DE
06 November 2014